LEONTYNE PRICE

Opera Superstar

by
Richard Steins

A BLACKBIRCH PRESS BOOK

WOODBRIDGE, CONNECTICUT

Published by Blackbirch Press, Inc.
One Bradley Road, Suite 205
Woodbridge, CT 06525

©1993 Blackbirch Press, Inc.
First Edition

Manufactured in the United States

10 9 8 7 6 5 4 3 2 1

Library of Congress Cataloging-in-Publication Data

Steins, Richard.
    Leontyne Price, opera superstar / by Richard Steins.—1st ed.
       p.   cm. — (The Library of famous women)
    Includes bibliographical references and index.
    Summary: A biography of the renowned soprano who helped break the
color barrier in professional opera during the 1960s.
    ISBN 0-56711-009-6
    1. Price, Leontyne—Juvenile literature. 2. Sopranos (Singers)—
United States—Biography—Juvenile literature. [1. Price, Leontyne.
2. Singers 3. Afro-Americans—Biography.] I. Title. II. Series.
ML3930.P745S73 1993
782.1'092—dc20
  [B]   92-40333
                                                            CIP
                                                          MN AC

Contents

Chapter 1

A Mississippi Childhood

Leontyne Price is a great American opera singer. Even though she was not the first African American to sing opera, she was the first to become a true superstar. Her career began in the 1950s and continues today. In addition to gaining fame for her highly praised performances of classical operatic characters, she has become well known in the United States and around the world through her television appearances and many recordings.

A Loving Family

Mary Violet Leontyne Price was born in the small town of Laurel, Mississippi, on February 10, 1927. She was the daughter of James Anthony Price and Katherine Baker Price. The timber industry was one of the major businesses in Laurel, and Leontyne's father worked for most of his life in the

(Opposite page)
Leontyne performed her final Metropolitan Opera role in 1985. When she was finished, the audience applauded for almost 30 minutes.

*
At an early age, Leontyne was witness to the beauty and power of music.

sawmills. In addition to raising a family, Leontyne's mother worked as a midwife, helping to deliver hundreds of babies in Laurel and the surrounding countryside.

Katherine Price was an amateur singer who sang in the choir of St. Paul's Methodist Church, where young Leontyne was witness to the beauty and power of music. Surrounded by music in church and at home, Leontyne revealed a remarkable musical talent from a young age. Before she was four years old, she began taking piano lessons with a teacher named Hattie McInnis. By the time Leontyne was five, her family was able to afford a piano for her to practice on at home. But it was her talent for singing that was quickly noticed by all who heard her.

When Leontyne was two years old, her brother, George, was born. Later, when they were grown up, both Leontyne and George recalled that their parents had provided a loving and supportive home life. According to Leontyne, her mother always gently advised her children to do their best at whatever they chose to do. The lesson was obviously helpful. As Leontyne became famous in the world of opera, George went on to become a general in the U.S. Army.

Early Challenges, Early Support

A black child born in the South in the 1920s faced many struggles. At that time, almost all of the South was strictly segregated (divided by race). Laurel, Mississippi, was no exception. Blacks lived on one side of town, and whites on the other. Blacks and whites went to separate churches and schools. Even though blacks and whites would have frequent contact with each other on a daily basis, they hardly ever socialized or became close friends. In and around the Laurel area, many blacks worked in the lumber industry, as did Leontyne's father. Some blacks were servants in the homes of the wealthy white people who lived on the north side of town.

Leontyne and her family lived on the south side of Laurel, where all the blacks lived. One member of the Price family—Leontyne's aunt, Everlina Greer—worked as a maid in the stately home of Alexander Chisholm. Mr. Chisholm was a wealthy white resident of Laurel. As a young child, Leontyne would often accompany her Aunt Everlina when she went to work at the Chisholm home. Alexander Chisholm and his wife, Elizabeth, had children of their own who were almost the same ages as Leontyne and her brother, George.

*

While Leontyne was growing up in the South, almost all the towns in the region were segregated.

Leontyne's gift for singing was recognized at an early age. When she was 17, she won a scholarship to attend Ohio's Central State University.

Because of these frequent visits, the Price children and the Chisholm children became friends, as did their parents. Leontyne's extraordinary musical talent was quickly noticed by Alexander and Elizabeth Chisholm. Leontyne was often asked to sing popular tunes at parties in the Chisholm home. In later years, when Leontyne went to school in New York City to continue with her musical studies, the Chisholm family helped pay her tuition at the Juilliard School.

As a teenager, Leontyne attended Oak Park Vocational High School. By now, the beauty of her voice had become widely known throughout Laurel, and Leontyne was asked to sing at most major musical occasions in town, including weddings and parties.

In 1944, at the age of 17, Leontyne won a scholarship to attend Central State University in Ohio. Traveling out of state for the first time presented different challenges to the talented young singer. Despite its racial segregation, Laurel had still provided a supportive environment in which Leontyne could develop her talents as a singer.

In the North, however, Leontyne met other kinds of barriers that she needed to overcome as she started her rise to worldwide fame. The North was segregated in a different way from the South. For example, the North did not *appear* to be as openly segregated as the South. Blacks did not have to use separate public facilities, nor were they denied access to hotels or restaurants that served white people. On the other hand, northern neighborhoods were segregated, and blacks were denied many opportunities for jobs and other kinds of advancement. In addition, as Leontyne's interest in opera grew, she would learn

✻

As a teenager, Leontyne was asked to sing at major musical occasions in Laurel, her hometown.

that even the operatic world was one that had been closed to black singers in many ways. If she was going to succeed, it would have to be on the sheer strength of her incredible talent.

Because of the supportive environment in which she grew up, Leontyne's childhood had prepared her for the challenges ahead. At a young age, she had no idea that she would eventually become an opera superstar. She knew, however, that she had a great gift for singing and that people loved to hear her perform. Her parents had always instilled confidence in her and urged her to pursue her talents. Even though she grew up in a segregated society, she had been able to mix with white people socially and to perform before black and white audiences. The young woman who went north to college in 1944 had two important qualities that would help to bring her great success. She had a beautiful voice and a strong determination to achieve her goals in life.

Chapter 2

A Singer Learns Her Art

At the age of 17, Leontyne traveled north by bus to attend Central State University in Wilberforce, Ohio. The year was 1944, and the United States was at war with Germany and Japan. African Americans were serving in large numbers in the armed forces, but the military, like most of the rest of the country, was segregated.

Living in Mississippi, Leontyne had seen firsthand the harsh realities of racial prejudice. She had experienced segregated neighborhoods and schools and had witnessed unfairness and insults toward African Americans. But she had also experienced the kindness of the Chisholm family and the early appreciation of both blacks and whites who had heard her perform for special occasions. It is perhaps for this reason that she had written on her college application, "I want so much to be a success."

At Central State, Leontyne began her studies as a music-education major. Everyone who heard her sing during those years, including teachers and classmates, urged her to focus on voice. Eventually, she switched her major to voice.

While at Central State, Leontyne decided that she wanted to attend the Juilliard School in New York City to continue her vocal studies. Juilliard is one of the most highly regarded music schools in the world. Many famous musicians and singers were once Juilliard students. Juilliard, however, was expensive. To raise money for Leontyne's tuition, the administration of Central State College helped set up a special benefit concert. The Chisholm family also generously gave Leontyne money to continue her education.

✳
Everyone at Central State who heard Leontyne sing urged her to focus her studies on voice.

The Juilliard School

Up to this point, Leontyne had sung only popular songs and had had little opportunity to see opera performed. But New York City was different. Even a poor student could afford to buy standing-room tickets to hear professional opera sung by the world's greatest singers. As a Juilliard student, Leontyne attended the New York City Opera and the Metropolitan Opera, where she would one day perform. Years later, Leontyne told an interviewer that she was swept away after hearing opera performed at the Met. It was inside that building that she finally realized she had to become an opera singer.

While she attended Juilliard, Leontyne studied with Florence Page Kimball. She was a voice coach who immediately recognized the great talent that Leontyne possessed. It became Florence Kimball's job to shape that talent. Kimball believed that Leontyne's voice, although deep in tone, should be trained for soprano roles. The soprano voice has the highest range. Traditionally, most of the greatest starring

The Juilliard School, in New York City, is one of the most highly respected music schools in the world.

roles for women in opera are written for the soprano voice.

Florence Page Kimball began to train Leontyne and to introduce her to various operatic roles. She concentrated on the operas of masters Giuseppe Verdi, Giacomo Puccini, and Wolfgang Amadeus Mozart. Leontyne's voice had a soothing, rich sound and was big in volume. Her deep sound had good quality in all its ranges, and she could sing high notes with ease.

With the right training, Kimball believed, Leontyne could sing almost anything in opera written for the soprano. However, the quality of Leontyne's voice was such that Italian opera seemed best suited to her. One of the most important things Kimball taught Leontyne was how to sing in such a way as to preserve her voice and not strain herself. It was a valuable lesson. Even during the 1990s, when she was in her mid-sixties, Leontyne still gave recitals and sang as well as ever.

The Juilliard School has an opera theater that offers public performances by the school's students. In one of her first major opera roles, Leontyne was cast as Mistress Ford in Verdi's *Falstaff.* This is not as large a role for a soprano as others written by Verdi. But it is an important part, requiring

*

As a student at the Juilliard School, Leontyne was "swept away" after hearing opera performed at the Met.

great vocal skill and acting ability. One day, Olin Downes, the music critic of *The New York Times*, was in the audience. Downes immediately recognized the truly superior quality of Leontyne's voice. She was, he believed, sure to be a future star.

Even while she performed at Juilliard, Leontyne continued to live the lean life of a student in New York. To earn extra money, she worked at the information desk in the dormitory residence of International House, where she lived. But while she struggled to make a name for herself, she was coming to the attention of influential people who believed in her ability to succeed.

First Opportunities

While singing Mistress Ford at Juilliard, Leontyne got her first opportunity for an important role in a major production. But it wasn't on the classical opera stage. The role was Bess in a new production of George Gershwin's folk opera, *Porgy and Bess*, which was written in the 1930s. This great musical work is about a group of poor African Americans living in a make-believe place called Catfish Row.

The producers of *Porgy and Bess*, Robert Breen and Blevins Davis, had heard about Leontyne. They attended a performance of

Falstaff at Juilliard and took with them the successful baritone, William Warfield. He had been cast in the male leading role of Porgy. After the performance, the three men went backstage to introduce themselves to Leontyne. This was Leontyne's first meeting with William Warfield, who later that year would become her husband.

Breen and Davis were very impressed by Leontyne's performance. Shortly after their visit, she accepted the role of Bess in their production.

Leontyne and William spent much time together during rehearsals for *Porgy and Bess,* **in which Leontyne had her first professional singing role.**

Rehearsals for *Porgy and Bess* began in May 1952. Davis and Breen wanted to take the opera on tour in the United States and

later travel with it throughout Europe. The plan then called for the production to return to the United States in 1953. It was to open in New York and then to be followed by another tour of the States.

Porgy and Bess's producers demanded two things for the production. They insisted that the cast be all black and that the opera not play before segregated audiences, even in the South. In addition, they persuaded the U.S. State Department to pay the expenses for part of the European tour.

Rehearsals were very tiring and time-consuming. During this busy but exciting period, Leontyne and William Warfield spent much time together, both on the set and off. Eventually, their personal relationship began to blossom.

At this time in their careers, William was the better-known artist. He had sung on the concert stage and had made his Hollywood debut in the popular movie *Showboat*. Leontyne, who had recently been just a student at Juilliard, was becoming more and more well known.

When the couple started dating seriously, William would frequently pick Leontyne up at her dormitory at International House. Years later, she told him that he was the "main attraction of I-House."

While singing a major role at Juilliard, Leontyne got her first opportunity to appear in a professional production.

Leontyne's classmates had always excitedly awaited her return from her dates with the "famous baritone."

Rave Reviews

Porgy and Bess opened its U.S. tour at the Dallas (Texas) State Fair in June 1952. From the first reviews, Leontyne began to understand what it would be like to be a famous person. The local critics almost immediately proclaimed her a star, and from that moment on, her life would never be the same. The *Dallas Morning News* reviewer, for example, wrote that Leontyne's voice had "purity, power, and impact."

Despite the rave reviews, the all-black cast faced long-standing discrimination, which was widespread in the South during the 1950s. Many members of the cast had trouble being seated in restaurants and making hotel reservations. For Leontyne, having grown up in the South, segregation was all too familiar.

From Dallas, the tour went to Chicago, Illinois. By this time, William had decided to propose to Leontyne. He invited her and two friends to an expensive restaurant in downtown Chicago. After ordering a bottle of champagne, William hoped to slip an engagement ring on Leontyne's finger while their hands were underneath the table. Instead, he dropped the ring on the floor! He and the two friends dived below the table to get it. Leontyne looked on curiously, but she probably knew what was coming.

After the ring was retrieved, William proposed—this time with both their hands on the tabletop. Leontyne accepted. A wedding date was set for August 31, 1952, shortly before the *Porgy and Bess* tour was to leave for Europe.

The last stop before Europe—and the wedding—was Washington, D.C. There, Leontyne was introduced to President Harry S. Truman and other government officials. They had come to wish the production company a fond farewell before it set off on its European tour.

One of Leontyne's first reviews described her voice as having "purity, power, and impact."

A Wedding and a Tour

Porgy and Bess soon closed at the National Theater in Washington. Leontyne and William, along with the entire cast of *Porgy*, boarded a chartered bus and headed north to New York City for the wedding. The marriage took place at the Abyssinian Baptist Church in Harlem. It was supposed to be performed by the Reverend Adam Clayton Powell, Jr., who was also a U.S.

congressman. However, Powell's car broke down on the way to the ceremony. So, Leontyne and William were married by the church's assistant pastor instead. From New York, they flew back to Washington D.C., in order to prepare for the European tour of *Porgy and Bess*.

The first stop in Europe was Vienna, Austria. The performance received rave reviews and a half-hour standing ovation from the audience. The tour then went on to Berlin, Germany; London, England; and Paris, France. The last stop was in February 1953.

Back to New York

After returning to the United States, Leontyne and the rest of the cast prepared for the big opening of *Porgy and Bess* in New York. It was scheduled for March 9, 1953, at the Ziegfeld Theater. The opening was a huge success and another triumph for Leontyne.

By this time, however, William had left the cast of *Porgy and Bess*. He had originally hoped to leave the tour after the London performances. He then wanted to return to the cast in New York to continue working with Leontyne throughout the second U.S. tour that was to follow in 1954.

(Opposite page)
On August 31, 1952, William and Leontyne took time out from their performances in *Porgy and Bess* to be married at the Abyssinian Baptist Church in New York City.

But because of scheduling problems that involved other commitments, William was forced to leave the production altogether. This meant that William and Leontyne faced a long period of separation while she continued in *Porgy* and he traveled across the country giving recitals.

Leontyne's young marriage was now at a crossroads. Her career seemed pointed in the direction of total opera stardom. And the stages of the country's opera houses were about to open for the first major black female artist in leading roles. Such was not the case, however, for William Warfield. Black male leads are, even today, a rarity in opera. These roles were even more rare in the 1950s. William had built a career on concert and musical stages and had also broken into film. He was not about to risk failure by trying to break the barrier to male black singers in opera's leading roles.

Still, on January 27, 1954, Leontyne and William gave their first joint recital at the Philadelphia Academy of Music. It turned out to be a rare moment. They would go on to sing together in recital only a few more times.

Despite their separations, Leontyne and William tried to make their marriage work.

In 1954, William found a house in New York City's Greenwich Village. The couple moved into it after Leontyne returned from the *Porgy* tour.

Having a house, however, did not help to strengthen Leontyne and William's marriage. Nor did it guarantee that the couple would be able to spend any more time together. After the *Porgy* tour, Leontyne was on the verge of another major breakthrough in her singing career—television. Television widened her audience. Now she would be known not only to ticket-buying theatergoers but also to millions of viewers all over the country. It would be through television that Leontyne would begin her final rise to total opera stardom.

On July 11, 1955, Leontyne and William were presented with awards from the National Association of Negro Musicians. Members of the organization honored them for "high artistic distinction throughout the world."

Chapter 3

Birth of a Superstar

Leontyne's first appearance on television came about through musical conductor Peter Herman Adler. He had heard Leontyne sing in *Porgy and Bess.* Adler was very impressed by Leontyne's voice. He was also convinced that she could sing the role of Floria Tosca in the opera *Tosca,* by Giacomo Puccini. This classical work was immensely popular and has become one of the most cherished operas.

Peter Adler was the conductor of an opera-theater orchestra whose televised performances of operas were seen nationwide by millions of opera fans. Leontyne was to appear before a huge audience to sing the role of a woman who was supposed to be white *and* Italian. This was truly a challenge for the time!

Today, audiences are more accustomed to seeing African Americans sing roles that

(Opposite page) **Leontyne gained great recognition for her portrayal of Aïda, the slave-princess, in Giuseppe Verdi's opera of the same name. It was a role that would become the "trademark" of her career.**

In 1955, Leontyne Price sang the role of Tosca in the opera of the same name by Giacomo Puccini. After a nationally televised performance of the opera, Leontyne was acclaimed for both her singing and acting skills.

were previously sung only by white people. Even the reverse is sometimes true. For example, in the role of Otello in the opera of the same name, we usually see a white singer in the role of a black man. In opera, the skin color of the singer has become totally unimportant. What matters is the singer's voice and performance.

This was not the case in 1955. In fact, NBC realized it was taking a big chance by having an African American sing the role of a white woman. Floria Tosca is supposed to be a Roman actress who is in love with a painter and political activist. Their stormy love affair takes place in Rome and is a dark story of politics, secrecy, betrayal, and murder.

NBC had a right to be concerned about casting Leontyne as Tosca. Before the broadcast, 11 southern cities announced that they would not televise the show. But the *Tosca* production went on as scheduled, and Leontyne enjoyed another triumph. The reviewer for *Time* magazine said that Leontyne's talent had almost "wiped out the color contrast between her and the other singers." The *Tosca* performance had demonstrated to millions that Leontyne was not only a magnificent singer but a wonderful dramatic actress as well.

After her national television debut, the
Metropolitan Opera in New York offered
Leontyne a contract to sing the title role in
Giuseppe Verdi's *Aïda*. This was a major
role in the country's leading opera house.
But Peter Adler and other friends advised
Leontyne not to accept the offer at that
point in her career. Adler believed that
Leontyne first needed to sing in other U.S.
opera houses and in Europe. Once she had
established herself throughout the United
States and overseas, she could sing at the
Met. At that later point, she would be an
even greater star, and she would be able to
demand more from the Met in terms of
singing roles.

Leontyne was faced with a difficult decision. The role of Aïda was ideally suited to
her voice. And the character was that of a
black Ethiopian princess enslaved by the
Egyptians in Egypt. As she was later to say,
"In *Aïda*, my skin is my costume."

*

*In 1955, NBC took
a big chance by
televising an opera
in which an
African American
sang the role of a
white woman.*

Debuts Abroad

Leontyne took the advice of her friends
and decided not to sing at the Met in 1955.
Instead, she sang more roles on television.
She also made successful debuts in opera
houses in the United States and Europe. As
Peter Adler had said, "Leontyne is to be a

In 1960, Leontyne made her debut at one of the world's most important opera houses, La Scala, in Milan, Italy. For her debut, Leontyne sang Aïda and was hailed by critics and audiences alike as a magnificent talent.

great artist. . . . When she makes her debut at the Met, she must do it as a lady, not as a slave." Adler was right. When Leontyne finally made her Met debut, it was as a lady in another Verdi opera. But she also sang the role of Aïda, the slave-princess. Aïda is the one role that Leontyne is most identified with.

In 1960, Leontyne made her debut at what many consider the most important opera house in the world—La Scala, in Milan, Italy. There, she sang the role of Aïda, and again her debut was a triumph.

Peter Adler's advice had been wise. Having first triumphed in other U.S. opera houses and in Europe, Leontyne was now ready for a truly spectacular debut at the Metropolitan Opera in New York City.

An opera singer is constantly in training. Even when she was not preparing for a role, Leontyne would practice every day, singing notes and doing other exercises to maintain the quality of her voice.

Preparing for a specific role, with all its words, notes, and movements, is very difficult. A new role can take years to learn. A singer first learns the part with a coach who accompanies him or her on the piano. As the opening performance draws near, rehearsals with the orchestra and the other singers in the opera begin.

Like most other great singers, Leontyne devoted almost all of her time to learning and practicing new roles. Sometimes she even relearned roles she had sung before. At times she would move out of her house and into a hotel during the months before the first performance. During these periods,

✳
Leontyne devoted almost all of her time to learning and practicing new roles.

her life consisted of three major things—
practicing, resting, and eating. A singer's
diet is very important, especially when
he or she is preparing for a role. Between
acts in the opera *La Forza del Destino* (The
Force of Destiny), for example, Leontyne
often had to eat a high-protein meal to
keep up her strength.

The public sees only the glamorous and
exciting parts of a famous singer's life—the
television appearances, the applause of the
audience, and the interviews with the news
media. The years and years of hard work
that go into learning a role are known only
by the performers and the people who are
close to them.

End of a Marriage

The house in New York City's Greenwich
Village became the place where Leontyne
and William spent whatever time they had
together. But both Leontyne and William
realized that much had changed in their
lives since their marriage in 1952. Now,
there was no denying that they were rarely
together because their careers had taken
them in different directions. And even
when they were both at home, Leontyne
might be deeply involved in preparing for
a new role and have little time to spend

with her husband. When Leontyne prepared for a part, she almost disappeared. For months before a new performance, her days would be spent rehearsing. There was no time left for parties or any other kind of socializing.

In addition, Leontyne was not the same person she had been in 1952. When she had stepped onto the stage to sing the role of Bess, she was barely out of school. She was not at all certain which direction her career should take. When she married William Warfield, he was not only slightly older, but he was also more experienced as

By 1958, the pressures of their professional lives had taken their toll on Leontyne and William's marriage. That year they separated; they did not divorce until 1972.

an artist. He could offer her advice and give guidance about which career moves to make. But now, Leontyne was a world-renowned star. She had her own agents and publicists and a new group of people to manage her career.

But more importantly, Leontyne herself had gained enormous confidence in her own abilities. She knew quite clearly the direction her career should follow. The singer's natural self-confidence that had first appeared in Laurel, Mississippi, continued to grow. As a student, she knew she had an excellent voice, but she didn't know what she would do with it. By the late 1950s, Leontyne was using her talent in the world of opera. She had succeeded beyond anyone's wildest dreams.

Sadly, both Leontyne and William also realized that their marriage had changed. In fact, it was no longer a marriage in the traditional sense. Being married means sharing common interests and goals and spending time together. Leontyne and William were on different paths. By 1958, they recognized their troubles and decided to separate. Their actual divorce did not come until 1972, but throughout the years, Leontyne and William remained close friends.

Chapter 4

A Career at the Met

On January 27, 1961, Leontyne Price stepped onto the stage of the Metropolitan Opera for the first time. That evening she was to sing the role of Leonora in *Il Trovatore* (The Troubadour) by Giuseppe Verdi. When the curtain came down about three hours later, the audience rose to its feet, cheering and applauding for more than 45 minutes.

A Historic Moment

It was one of the greatest debuts in Met history, and a historic moment. Only one week before—on January 20—President John F. Kennedy had been sworn into office in Washington, D.C. The new president promised to advance civil rights for African Americans. Leontyne's years of fame were beginning just at the time when the civil rights movement would firmly establish itself in America.

A debut at the Metropolitan Opera is one of the most important milestones in any opera singer's career. The Met is the major opera house in the United States. But it is also one of the finest in the world. A Metropolitan debut meant even more to someone like Leontyne, who was an African American. Until the 1950s, blacks had never sung at the Met. It simply wasn't done, and there was much resistance to allowing it, especially by the Met's traditional board of directors.

But in 1950, Rudolf Bing became the Met's general manager. In 1955, he hired Marian Anderson, the first African American to sing at the Met.

At the time of her Met debut, Marian Anderson was already 52 years old. She was a beloved and historic figure in American music. Anderson had achieved instant fame in 1939, when an organization called the Daughters of the American Revolution (DAR) refused to allow her to perform at Constitution Hall in Washington, D.C., because she was black. Eleanor Roosevelt, the wife of President Franklin D. Roosevelt, was outraged. She invited Marian Anderson to sing instead at the Lincoln Memorial. More than 75,000 people attended the outdoor Easter recital.

(Opposite page) **Marian Anderson was the first African American to sing at the Metropolitan Opera. Her debut paved the way for Leontyne Price, who idolized Marian Anderson and was inspired by Anderson's debut at the Met.**

Leontyne's first role at the Metropolitan Opera was noblewoman Leonora in Giuseppe Verdi's opera *Il Trovatore*. She is shown here in a performance of *Il Trovatore* that was later broadcast on NBC.

Despite the drama surrounding her life, Anderson was a shy and private woman. She had made her career through singing recitals, and not through dramatic roles on the stage. The operatic roles in her vocal range (contralto) are usually not starring roles like the parts written for sopranos. At the Met, Marian Anderson sang the role of Ulrica, a dark-skinned sorceress in Verdi's *Un Ballo in Maschera* (A Masked Ball). She sang only light performances and never appeared at the Met again. But her mark in history was made—she had shattered a racial barrier.

The 28-year-old Leontyne Price was in the audience to hear her idol, Marian Anderson, make her Met debut. Filled with pride, Leontyne was deeply moved and inspired by Anderson's triumph.

When Leontyne finally made her own Met debut, she was 33 years old and in excellent vocal condition. Her first role at the Met was the noblewoman Leonora in Verdi's *Il Trovatore*. In the end, this character takes her own life because of her love for a gypsy named Manrico. The part of Leonora is extremely difficult to sing. But Leontyne carried the day and received rave reviews. The Italian tenor Franco Corelli made his Metropolitan debut that same evening, singing Manrico. With all the attention focused on Leontyne, Corelli complained, "I never want to sing with that soprano again!" In the future, however, he would sing many more times with Leontyne and would publicly recognize her as a remarkable talent.

In the audience that night were the New York critics and fans of opera. In addition, Leontyne's parents; her brother, George; and Alexander and Elizabeth Chisholm had journeyed north from Mississippi. They wanted to share the proud moment with Laurel's most famous daughter.

✳

In Il Trovatore, *Leontyne carried the day and received rave reviews.*

The OPERA Masters

During her career, Leontyne Price sang roles from many different operas in many different languages. Most of her time at the Metropolitan Opera was spent singing the great classical roles of opera, demanding roles that are the true tests for professionals. These classical roles, composed by musical geniuses such as Mozart, Tchaikovsky, Puccini, and Verdi, are performed by almost every female singer who wants to become a superstar in the world of opera. Photos of famous opera composers, accompanied by the names of some of their best-known works are included on these two pages.

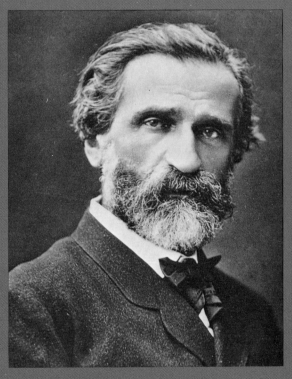

Giuseppe Verdi (1813–1901) was born in Italy. Among his many famous operas are *Il Trovatore* (The Troubador, 1853), *Un Ballo in Maschera* (A Masked Ball, 1859), and *Aïda* (1871).

(Inset above) Wolfgang Amadeus Mozart (1756–1791) was born in Austria. By the age of 10, he had published more than eight violin sonatas and two symphonies. Among his many famous operas are *The Marriage of Figaro* (1786), *Don Giovanni* (1787), *Cosi Fan Tutte* (All Women Are Like That, 1790) and *The Magic Flute* (1791).

Peter Ilyich Tchaikovsky (1840–1893) was born in Russia. Included among his many famous compositions is the opera *Eugene Onegin* (1879).

George Gershwin (1896–1983) was born in the United States. One of his many famous operatic compositions is *Porgy and Bess* (1935).

Giacomo Puccini (1858–1924) was born in Italy. His many famous operas include *La Bohème* (1896), *Tosca* (1900), *Madama Butterfly* (1904), *La Fanciulla del West* (The Girl of the Golden West, 1910), and *Turandot* (completed by Franco Alfano).

Leontyne appeared with opera star Cesare Siepi in a televised version of Mozart's *Don Giovanni* in 1962.

Met Showcase

That first season at the Met turned out to be a showcase for the most famous roles that Leontyne would sing throughout her career. On February 20, she sang Aïda on the stage of the Met for the first time. Two weeks later, on March 3, she sang the lead role of Cio-Cio-San in Giacomo Puccini's *Madama Butterfly.* Her performance of the gentle but cunning Japanese geisha who is betrayed by an American naval lieutenant was truly dramatic. It was sharply different from the noblewoman and slave-princess she had portrayed in her first two Met roles. As usual, Leontyne brought to the part outstanding vocal ability and a uniquely sensitive interpretation.

On March 25, 1961, she first sang the role of Donna Anna in Mozart's *Don Giovanni.* This time, she portrayed a noble lady who eagerly wanted punishment for the man who had murdered her father. The final new role of Leontyne's first season at the Met was Liu, another slave girl, in Puccini's *Turandot,* set in China.

The first season at the Met had shown the wide range of characters and musical styles that Leontyne was able to perform. In the 1960s, as it had done since 1883, the Met took its performances on tour to various

(Opposite page)
Leontyne first sang the role of Cio-Cio-San in Puccini's *Madama Butterfly* on March 3, 1961.

cities around the United States. Rudolf Bing, the Met's general manager, had a long-standing policy of refusing to play before segregated audiences. The addition of Leontyne to the Met's cast meant that she, as a popular new soprano, would be touring with the Met as it traveled around the country. This, of course, included the South.

In 1961, most public buildings were still segregated throughout the South. Rudolf Bing was determined to protect Leontyne and any other cast members from the humiliation of discrimination. When the tour arrived in Atlanta, Georgia, Bing made a bold public statement. He entered the hotel dining room with Leontyne on his arm. As he relates in his memoirs, a hush fell over the room. But Bing, and perhaps also Leontyne, derived much satisfaction from the moment.

Rudolf Bing was personally careful to protect Leontyne from the prejudice and discrimination of the time, especially when the company was traveling on tour. But it was very difficult for a large, integrated company to travel anywhere in the United States before the civil rights revolution of the 1960s. Black members of the company had to stay in hotels for blacks only. They

*

Even as an established star of professional opera, Leontyne experienced discrimination and the ugliness of prejudice.

were also not allowed to eat in restaurants that served whites. Leontyne had met with this kind of discrimination while growing up in Mississippi, but even as a famous opera singer, she was not excluded from the ugliness of prejudice.

A Period of Rest

One of the most treasured events for any Met singer is to be part of an opening-night production. Opening night at the Met is the beginning of the opera season. It is a great social event, with powerful and famous figures appearing at the opera house in their finest clothing. In a sense, the Met opening night is also the beginning of the fall and winter social season in New York City.

As the Met's newest star, Leontyne was asked to open the 1961–1962 season in Puccini's *La Fanciulla del West* (The Girl of the Golden West). More racial barriers were broken on this night. It was the first time an African American was opening the Met season. It was also the first time that the role of Minnie was being sung by a black woman. *La Fanciulla del West* is an Italian opera. However, it is set in the American West during the nineteenth century and has a Wild West theme.

For a while it seemed that the season would not open at all. There was a threat of a strike on the part of the Met's labor unions. Leontyne had spent the summer of 1961 in Europe. During that time, she had appealed to President John F. Kennedy and his labor secretary, Arthur Goldberg, to help settle things between the unions and the Met management. Eventually, all the various disagreements were settled, and the season went on as scheduled.

The year 1961 had been an incredible success for Leontyne. First there was her Met debut, followed by four additional roles sung in just two months. Then there was the opening night of the new season with its many pressures. All this proved to be too much for Leontyne. During one of the later performances of *La Fanciulla del West*, Leontyne lost her voice from a viral infection. Although she tried to sing, no sound came out. Despite this, Leontyne bravely continued to act the role until a replacement singer could be found, but she was clearly not well and needed a rest.

On orders from her doctor, Leontyne gave up further performances in the show. In December 1961, she left for Rome for a period of rest. She returned to the Met in April 1962 for her second season. She sang

The Metropolitan Opera was located on 39th Street in New York City until it moved uptown to Lincoln Center in 1966.

the role of Tosca, which she had originally performed on television in 1955.

Her illness in late 1961 taught Leontyne that she needed to start pacing herself more carefully. Florence Page Kimball, her teacher at Juilliard, had always stressed the importance of not overdoing it. Now that she was an internationally established star, Leontyne was in tremendous demand by opera houses all over America and Europe. If she was to avoid overworking herself and risking illness, she had to learn to choose her roles carefully. During her third season at the Met (1962–1963), Leontyne sang only one new role, Elvira, in Verdi's *Ernani.* The rest of the season she performed roles that she had sung before.

Between 1963 and 1965, Leontyne sang two new Mozart roles, Pamina in *The Magic Flute* and Fiordiligi in *Così Fan Tutte* (All Women Are Like That). She added one part, Tatiana, from the Russian opera *Eugene Onegin* by Peter Ilyich Tchaikovsky.

A Closing and an Opening

A new and great honor awaited Leontyne in 1966. That year was to be the final year that the Metropolitan Opera performed in the old opera house on 39th Street in New York City. In September, the company was

Leontyne visited her hometown of Laurel, Mississippi a number of times during her long career. Here, she gives a recital in front of an integrated audience of more than 2,000 people in 1963. Leontyne's proud parents are sitting in the front row, third and fourth from the left.

scheduled to move into a newer and larger building at Lincoln Center, which was farther uptown. The new building was an impressive structure, with stained-glass windows in the front. A gala farewell was held at the old Met on April 17, 1966. Leontyne was one of many Metropolitan Opera stars to sing that night.

After the performance, Leontyne was selected to take part in an unusual ceremony. The old Met stage curtain would not be going uptown to the new theater. Instead, it was going to be cut up into 45,000 small pieces. These tiny bits of cloth would be included in a special record album of Met opening nights produced by RCA Victor. At the ceremony, Leontyne took a pair of shears and cut the first piece out of the old curtain.

In 1966, the Metropolitan Opera moved to New York City's newest and greatest center for the arts: Lincoln Center.

To celebrate the move to Lincoln Center, the Met asked the American composer, Samuel Barber, to write a new opera. It was called *Antony and Cleopatra.* Based on the play by William Shakespeare, it told the story of the powerful love affair between the Egyptian queen and the Roman general. Leontyne was chosen to sing the leading role of Cleopatra.

On September 27, 1966, *Antony and Cleopatra* opened the Met season in the new opera house. The staging was a disaster, and the production was poorly received by almost all the critics. They agreed that it was overdone—the sets, the costumes, the live animals, and the moving pyramids. In one scene, for example, there

Leontyne gets a kiss backstage from co-star Justino Diaz. They had just finished their performance in *Antony and Cleopatra,* which was the first opera to open at the new Metropolitan Opera in Lincoln Center.

were 3 horses, 2 camels, 1 elephant, and
165 people on stage! The music and singing were almost lost. Moreover, during the
rehearsals, Leontyne had got stuck in a
pyramid that refused to open, and she
could barely walk in her heavy costumes.

Although the opera was not a success,
Leontyne had sung beautifully. She later
recorded one of the arias from the opera.
To open the Met in its new quarters and
in a new opera was still an honor for
Leontyne. The honor was given to her in
recognition of her status with the Met
audiences and in the world of opera.

A Decade of Success

By 1971, only 10 years after her Met
debut, Leontyne had already sung a total
of 146 performances at the Met and had
played 14 roles. She was unquestionably
one of the biggest box-office draws.
Leontyne also recorded almost all of the
roles that she had sung at the Met and
elsewhere. Most of these recordings are
still available in stores that sell classical
music. They are a permanent testimony
to her art over the years. And they are a
way for those who never saw her perform
on stage to at least hear the timeless beauty
of her voice.

**During her first 10 years
with the Metropolitan
Opera, Leontyne had
played 14 major roles
and had given a total of
146 performances.**

*

Leontyne wanted to leave the opera while her voice was still in top form.

The 1970s brought a significant change in Leontyne's career. There were now longer periods between appearances in operas. Her Met performances grew fewer. Often, seasons would go by in which she did not star in any major operas. Instead, Leontyne began devoting more time to recitals, to concerts, and to resting before and after all performances. When she did return to the opera stage, she was always greeted with thunderous applause. It was an expression of the love of her audiences.

In 1977, Leontyne turned 50. Although she was now middle-aged, her voice was still remarkably youthful and unchanged. She continued to pace herself and to choose her roles and public appearances with care. But the time was approaching when Leontyne would need to make a decision about retiring from the opera stage. Leontyne wanted to leave opera while her voice was still in top form. Nothing would be worse, she believed, than to stay too long.

Leontyne's farewell from opera was to be as dramatic as her entrance onto the stage of the Met.

Chapter 5

A Superstar
Retires

For Leontyne's final
Metropolitan Opera
performance, she chose
to appear in the role of
Aïda. This was the part
with which she had
become most identified
and the one that meant the most to her.
In an interview in the magazine *Opera News*
in 1985, Leontyne spoke about the character of Aïda:

> Aïda is a very personal role for me. She is
> where I am, often, as a woman. . . . You are
> presenting a woman as you would yourself.
> . . . There's something about her that is
> provocative, and on that kernel of feeling I
> build my character of Aïda.

As with her debut in 1961, Leontyne's
departure in 1985 was both historic and
moving. The performance was carried live
on the Public Broadcasting Service (PBS)
television network. At times, it was both a
physically demanding and emotionally
trying event for Leontyne. When the

Leontyne as Leonora in
Giuseppe Verdi's
Il Trovatore.

52

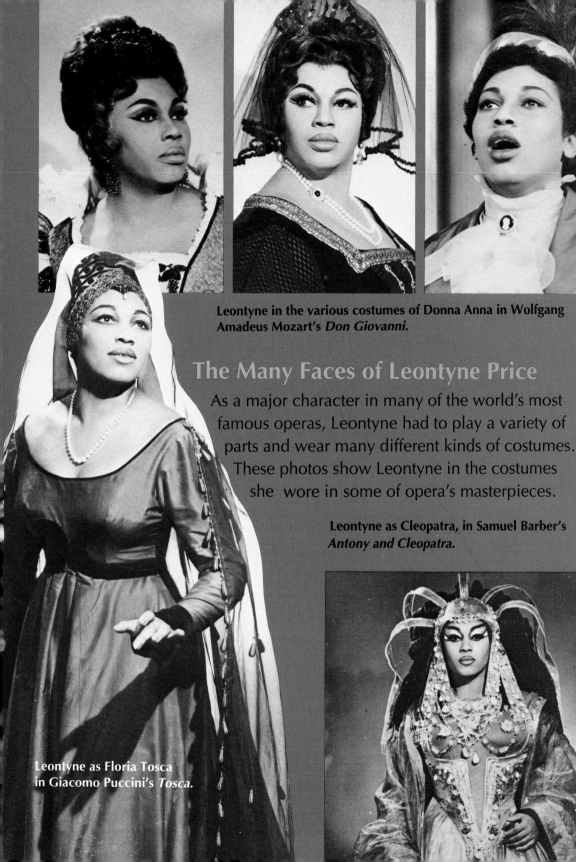

Leontyne in the various costumes of Donna Anna in Wolfgang Amadeus Mozart's *Don Giovanni*.

The Many Faces of Leontyne Price

As a major character in many of the world's most famous operas, Leontyne had to play a variety of parts and wear many different kinds of costumes. These photos show Leontyne in the costumes she wore in some of opera's masterpieces.

Leontyne as Cleopatra, in Samuel Barber's *Antony and Cleopatra*.

Leontyne as Floria Tosca in Giacomo Puccini's *Tosca*.

applause and cheering went on and on at the end of the opera, she bowed her head, close to tears.

But there were no regrets. She had left the stage in peak vocal condition. From this point on, she could devote all of her attention to occasional recitals, to teaching young opera singers of the future, and to tending the garden at her New York City house on Vandam Street.

Enjoying Life, Helping Others

Although her performing career was behind her, Leontyne remained active in music, and she even continued to give recitals. In her programs, she sang spirituals, art songs, selections from operas, popular songs, and Broadway show tunes. Her large audiences remained as enthusiastic as ever.

The advantage of giving recitals was that she could pick and choose the dates and places. This allowed her ample time to prepare for performances and to relax after them.

In 1990, Leontyne undertook another new project when she published a book, titled *Aïda: A Picture Book for All Ages, As Told by Leontyne Price*. Although much had been written about Leontyne over the course of her career, she had never written an autobiography. The book showed her appreciation of the opera that in many ways had become her "signature piece."

Leontyne gave two recitals in the city of Naples, Florida, in January 1992. Her program was made up of old favorites—among them an aria from *Madama Butterfly*. It also included a series of songs by the American composer Lee Hoiby. Though it is a small place, Naples has a beautiful new concert hall and a large symphony orchestra. It was

At the tenth annual National Theater Awards in 1987, Leontyne was given an award for her achievements in opera.

Leontyne chatted with her idol, Marian Anderson, after performing for a huge crowd at Carnegie Hall in 1987. The performance was a benefit for the United Negro College Fund.

an ideal setting for Leontyne to relax and enjoy singing without the high pressure of a staged operatic performance. These recitals, given when Leontyne was just shy of her sixty-fifth birthday, showed once again how youthful and flexible her voice still was.

Teaching assumed an important place in Leontyne's life after the Met as well. Her enjoyment of it came as something of a surprise. She often gave what are known as master classes. These are classes in which talented voice students perform an aria or musical piece before a famous singer. The singer then reviews the performance and offers advice on the use of voice and interpretation of the piece.

Leontyne also discovered that she had become a kind of mother figure to a new generation of talented black singers who had followed in her footsteps in the opera world. These younger people would often visit her at her home in New York City. There, she would offer them advice and guidance on their careers. All in all, Leontyne found much joy in her life after the Met. Even though she was no longer an active Met star, she still enjoyed the awe and respect of all who knew of her work.

*

Today, Leontyne is still considered one of the greatest operatic sopranos of the twentieth century.

The Importance of Leontyne Price

Today, Leontyne Price is thought of as one of the greatest operatic sopranos of the twentieth century. The fact that she is an African American is unimportant to her success in the world of opera. But the fact is that she is black, and she did come from a segregated town in Mississippi. She conquered the heights of opera in the United States and Europe. There were black opera singers long before Leontyne started her career. But very few of them achieved the fame they deserved.

Why did this situation change during Leontyne's career? It was mostly because, at the time, the United States was in the middle of a great revolution in civil rights. The doors of previously segregated institutions were opened to African Americans. Eventually, even opera yielded and gave African Americans their rightful place on the stage. But even the great Marian Anderson was not permitted to use the front entrance of the St. Regis Hotel at the time she made her historical debut at the Met.

Marian Anderson was followed by a few other black singers. These included sopranos Martina Arroyo and Mattiwilda Dobbs in the late 1950s. But it was Leontyne Price who arrived at the Met as an already established star. She came as one who clearly understood—and did not apologize for—her superstar status. She had worked hard, and she knew she deserved recognition.

With wise advice, Leontyne had carefully managed her career to make the strongest impression. For example, when she turned down the Met's first offer to sing in *Aïda*, she was taking a gamble. By delaying her debut in that famous and important opera house, Leontyne hoped to arrive as a greater star in a more powerful position. In the end, she did exactly that.

(Opposite page)
Leontyne received a lifetime-achievement award at the 1989 Grammy Awards.

Leontyne once said that her role in the civil rights movement was just in "being" black. She did not march in demonstrations or take public positions on important political issues. Instead, she helped the advancement of civil rights simply through her immense talent and by her mere presence in the public eye. In this sense, her contribution was unique and will always be remembered.

Glossary
Explaining New Words

aria A song for a single voice, included in operas and other musical works.

baritone A category of singing voice in men; describes a deep, low voice.

contralto A category of singing voice in women; describes the lowest end of the voice range.

debut A first appearance.

Juilliard School A music school in New York City known for training talented musicians, composers, and singers.

La Scala An important opera house located in Milan, Italy.

Lincoln Center In New York City, a group of six buildings for the performing arts; the home of the Metropolitan Opera since 1966.

Metropolitan Opera The major opera house of the United States, located in New York City.

opera A play set to music, with words sung and sometimes spoken to the music of an orchestra.

recital An informal musical performance, usually of a classical work.

soprano A category of singing voice in women; describes the highest end of the voice range.

tenor A category of singing voice in men; describes the high end of the voice range.

For Further Reading

Blackwood, Alan. *Music.* Milwaukee: Raintree Steck-Vaughn, 1990.

Carlin, Richard. *European Classical Music 1600-1825.* New York: Facts On File, 1988.

Clark, Elizabeth. *Tchaikovsky.* New York: Franklin Watts, 1988.

Mordden, Ethan. *Demented: The World of the Opera Diva.* New York: Franklin Watts, 1984.

Sabin, Francene. *Mozart, Young Music Genius.* Mahwah, NJ: Troll Books, 1990.

Young, Percy. *Mozart.* New York: Franklin Watts, 1988.

Index

Photo Credits:
Cover: Metropolitan Opera Archives; p.4: AP/Wide World Photos; pp. 5, 8, 11, 16, 25, 26, 31, 49, 51: Schomburg Center for Research in Black Culture/New York Public Library; p.13 ©Henry Grossman/Courtesy Communications Office, The Juilliard School; p.21: AP/Wide World Photos; p. 23: AP/Wide World Photos; p.24: Metropolitan Opera Archives; p.28: AP/Wide World Photos; p.33: AP/Wide World Photos; p.35: AP/Wide World Photos; p.36: AP/Wide World Photos; pp.38-39: Culver Pictures; p.41: Metropolitan Opera Archives; p.44: Metropolitan Opera Archives; p.46: AP/Wide World Photos; p.47: ©Bruce Glassman/Blackbirch Press; p.48: AP/Wide World Photos; p.52: Metropolitan Opera Archives; p.53: (top left and top center) Metropolitan Opera Archives, (top right) Schomburg Center for Research in Black Culture/New York Public Library, (below left) Metropolitan Opera Archives, (below right) Schomburg Center for Research in Black Culture/New York Public Library; p.55: AP/Wide World Photos; p.56: AP/Wide World Photos; p.59: AP/Wide World Photos.

Photo research by Grace How.